Jesus Said, "Go and Tell!"

Matthew 28:16–20 for children

Written by Kari Vo
Illustrated by Susan Spellman

CONCORDIA PUBLISHING HOUSE · SAINT LOUIS

When Jesus rose up from the dead,
He went to meet His friends;
For forty days, He talked with them
And shared with them His plans.

He sent them to a mountain side, up
Away in Galilee,
And when He met them at that place,
He said, "Listen to Me:

"My Father said these words to Me:
'I give to You all might,
All rule, and all authority
To do as You see right.'"

"'All creatures in the heavens above
And on the earth below
Shall do God's will and honor Him
And at His bidding go.'

"And that's the reason why I say
You have a job to do;
Today, I'll tell you what I've planned,
The work I have for you.

"I call you all My followers,
Disciples whom I love;
I gave My life so you could live
With Me in heaven above."

"But you are not the only ones
I want to be My own;
I want to see the whole world stand,
Rejoicing at God's throne.

"Go out into the whole wide world,
Every tribe and nation,
To every country, every land,
All God's good creation."

HOLY BIBLE

"Go to all people everywhere,
And tell them about Me;
Give them the gift I gave to you:
Disciples they will be.

"Tell them the story: how God came
To be a man like them,
To live, to suffer, and to die
And then to rise again."

"Tell them that all who trust in Me
Have their sins forgiven;
They're God's children here on earth and
Evermore in heaven.

"Give them the Word I gave to you:
Baptize them in the name
Of Father, Son, and Spirit, who
Removes all sin and shame.

"Teach them to treasure My commands
And everything I say;
Give them My Word so they may trust
And know God's living way."

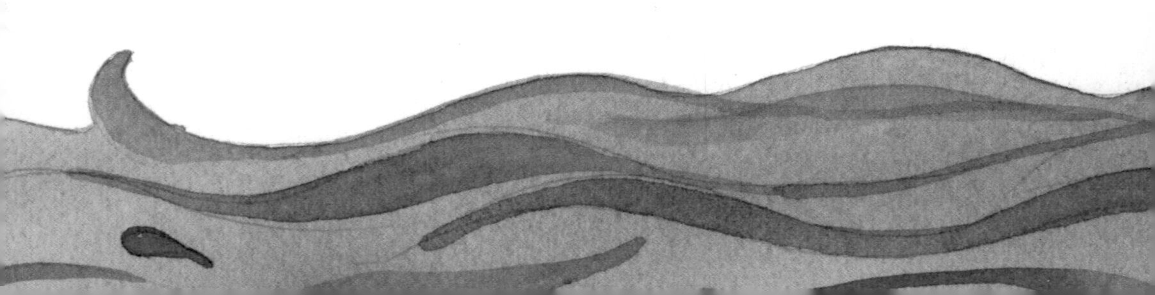

“And I am with you—don’t forget!
I won’t leave you alone;
I’ll stay with you until you stand
Before My heavenly throne.

“Until the heavens and the earth
Shall fade and pass away;
Until the day that I return
To take you home to stay.”

So Jesus spoke and then returned
To be with God in heaven;
His followers rejoiced to hear
His Great Commission given.

He told us "Go!" and so we go
To neighbors far and near
To share the wonderful Good News
That takes away our fear.